KIDS AROUND THE WORLD

KIDS IN MEXICO

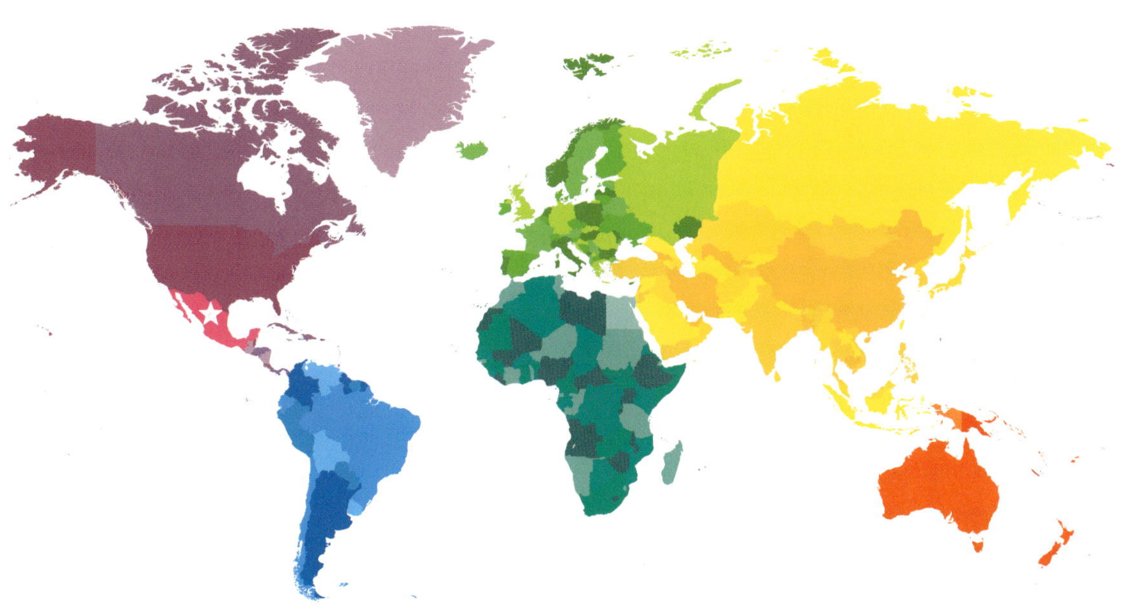

by Nikki Potts Ferguson

PEBBLE
a capstone imprint

Published by Pebble, an imprint of Capstone
1710 Roe Crest Drive, North Mankato, Minnesota 56003
capstonepub.com

Library of Congress Cataloging-in-Publication Data is available on the Library of Congress website.

ISBN: 9798875247972 (hardcover)
ISBN: 9798875247927 (paperback)
ISBN: 9798875247934 (ebook PDF)

Summary: Outstanding photographs and easy-to-understand text describe Mexico's landmarks, holidays, sports, foods, transportation, and more.

Editorial Credits
Editor: Erika L. Shores; Designer: Sarah Bennett; Media Researcher: Rebekah Hubstenberger; Production Specialist: Tori Abraham

Image Credits
Dreamstime: © Carlos Araujo, 15; Getty Images: aldomurillo, cover (bottom), FG Trade Latin, 9, 12, Hector Vivas, 26, iStock/bonchan, 18, iStock/EvaLepiz, 25, iStock/SK Lafoca, 6, Jeff J Mitchell, 14, Laura Olivas, 13, M Swiet Productions, 16, Manuel Velasquez, 23, Photo ©Tan Yilmaz, 17, Photo Beto, 27, Rick Gomez, 19, Rob Tilley, cover (top), Toya Sarno Jordan, 22; Newscom: Benedicte Desrus/Sipa USA, 10; Shutterstock: Aberu.Go, 7, Clau Stavros, 5, Globe Turner, 29, Jojo Textures (rainbow border), cover and throughout, la.la.land, cover (globe icon), lunamarina, 20, Miguel Angel Bistrain, 21, Pyty, back cover, 1, 4, Roaming Pictures, 28

Capstone thanks Ana Laura González, Mexico City, Mexico, for her assistance in creating this book.

Printed and bound in Malaysia. 006460

TABLE OF CONTENTS

Words in **bold** are in the glossary.

WELCOME TO MEXICO

Mexico is a country in southern North America. It has many kinds of **landscapes**. There are beaches, deserts, jungles, mountains, and more.

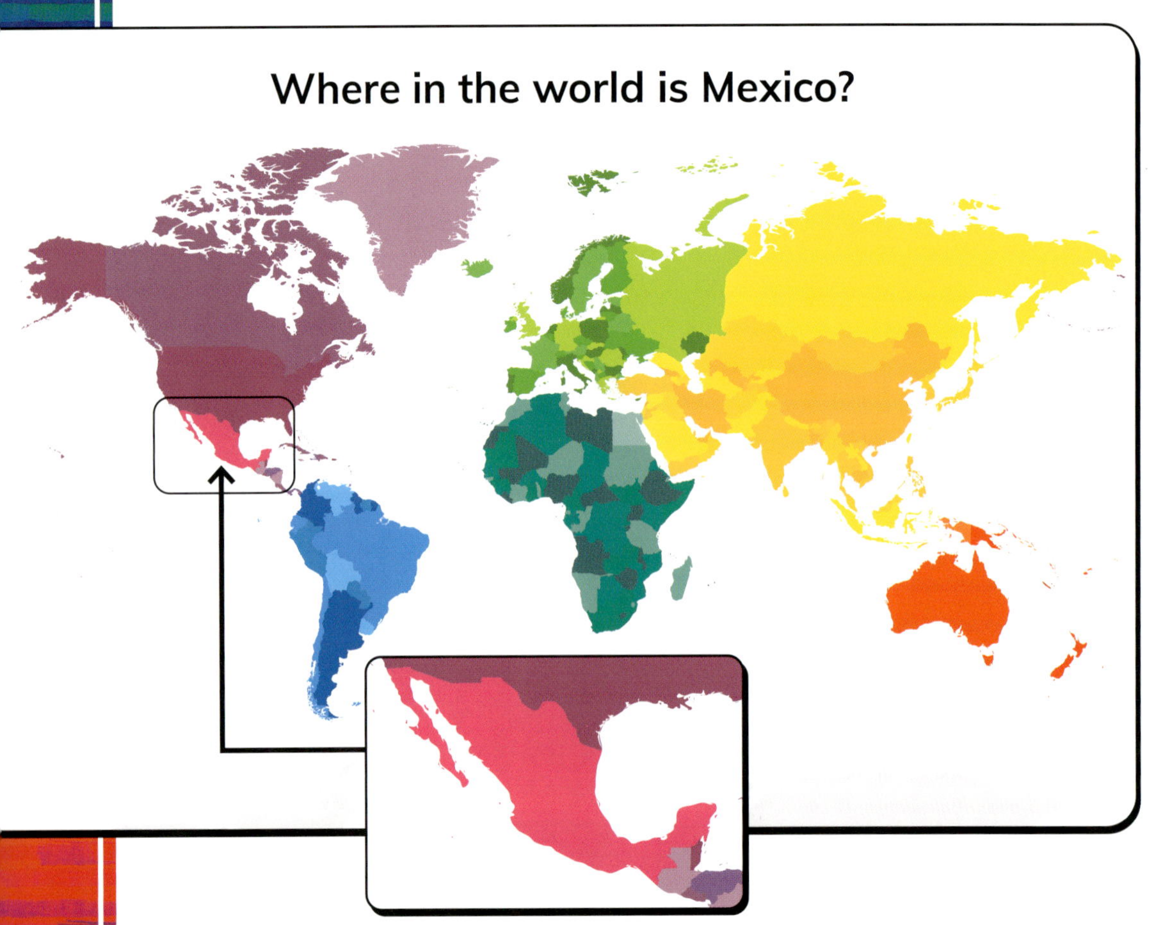

People have lived in Mexico for at least 10,000 years. Today, more than 130 million people live in the country. Let's learn what life is like for kids in Mexico.

AT HOME

Most people in Mexico live in towns or cities. Some live in **rural** areas. Many families live in houses. People also live in apartments and condos.

In Mexico, most kids live with their parents and siblings. Some homes also include other family members, like grandparents, aunts, and uncles. Families in Mexico are often tight-knit. They live close together and see each other often.

TRAVEL AND SCHOOL

Many kids in Mexico go to public school. Others attend private school. Students at public schools wear **uniforms**.

Some kids ride the bus to school. A friend or family member might give students a ride to school. Kids may also walk or ride their bikes.

private school bus

Bienestar Escolar

Kids in Mexico start elementary school at age 6. At age 12, they go to junior high school. High school is from ages 15 to 18. At school, kids learn Spanish, math, history, science, art, and more.

For many students, the school year is from August to July. Many school days are split into two sessions. Students might go to school either in the morning or in the afternoon.

FUN AND GAMES

Many kids in Mexico enjoy dance and music classes. They like outdoor activities such as jump rope. They also play card games and board games.

Lotería is a traditional Mexican game. Each player has a board with different images. A caller draws a card from a deck. If the card matches a picture on a player's board, they mark it. The person who first gets four marks in a row wins the game.

Sports such as basketball, boxing, tennis, and golf are often played in Mexico. Fútbol is the most popular sport. In some countries, fútbol is known as soccer.

Kids in Mexico play fútbol through school teams or in clubs. They might play with friends in their neighborhoods.

Kids and their families enjoy going to Mexico's beautiful beaches. They swim and fish. They might see sea turtles!

El Tajín

Families might also visit some of Mexico's historic sites. Uxmal and Chichén Itzá are **ruins** of ancient Mayan cities. Aztec **pyramids** can be found at El Tajín.

FOOD IN MEXICO

Many traditional foods are still eaten in Mexico today. Tacos have been eaten in the country for hundreds of years. Flat, corn tortillas are fried and shaped like a "U." They are filled with spiced meats, cheeses, and vegetables.

tacos

enchiladas

Enchiladas are corn tortillas filled with meats, cheeses, and vegetables. They are rolled and then baked. Seafood is popular in areas near the coasts.

Spicy gummy candies and chocolate are popular sweets. Candies come in many flavors such as mango, honey, pineapple, and lemon. Tamarind is a popular flavor. Pan de Muerto is a sweet bread made during the holiday Día de los Muertos.

Mazapán is made of peanuts and sugar. It is formed into a round flat shape. People eat it plain. They might also use it in other desserts.

LET'S CELEBRATE!

Día de los Muertos is a Mexican holiday. It is celebrated on November 1 and 2. People honor friends and family who have died.

Kids help their families make offerings. They might put food, flowers, and pictures on an **altar** for their loved one. Families dance and listen to music. People visit cemeteries. On November 2, a big parade is held in Mexico City.

Guelaguetza is a holiday celebrated in Oaxaca, Mexico. It is celebrated at the end of July for two weeks.

People from different ethnic groups in the area come together. They bring bread, sweets, and other gifts. They share parts of their **culture** such as clothing, language, and music.

Mexican Independence Day takes place on September 16. It celebrates Mexico's independence from Spain. Today, kids and their families watch fireworks.

Across the country, people go to parades and celebrations. They might dance and listen to **mariachi** bands. People decorate with green, white, and red. These are the colors of the Mexican flag.

Mexico is rich with culture. Millions of people visit the country each year. People of all ages enjoy the food, historical places, and beautiful beaches. Ancient ruins, mazapán, and fútbol await in Mexico!

FAST FACTS

Location: Southern North America

Capital: Mexico City

Population: 130,739,927 people

Size: 758,449 square miles
(1.96 million square kilometers)

Official Language: Spanish

Currency: Mexican peso

GLOSSARY

altar (AWL-tuhr)—a raised platform or table used for worship

culture (KUHL-chuhr)—a people's way of life, ideas, art, customs, and traditions

landscape (LAND-skayp)—the form of the land in a particular area

mariachi (mah-ree-AH-chee)—having to do with the traditional music played by a Mexican street band

pyramid (PIHR-uh-mid)—a solid building with sloping sides that come together at the top

ruins (ROO-ins)—the remains of a building or other things that have fallen down or been destroyed

rural (RUR-uhl)—having to do with the countryside

uniform (YOON-uh-form)—special clothes that members of a group wear

READ MORE

Gómez, Isela Xitlali, and Anaïs Deal-Márquez. *Your Passport to Mexico*. North Mankato, MN: Capstone, 2022.

O'Neill, Sean. *50 Things You Didn't Know about Mexico*. Minneapolis: Lerner, 2025.

INTERNET SITES

Britannica Kids: Mexico
kids.britannica.com/kids/article/Mexico/345743

Globe Trottin' Kids: Mexico
globetrottinkids.com/countries/mexico/

National Geographic Kids: Mexico
kids.nationalgeographic.com/geography/countries/article/mexico

INDEX

ABOUT THE AUTHOR

Nikki Potts Ferguson is a children's author and editor. Besides writing, she enjoys reading, crafting, and spending time with her family. Nikki lives in Kentucky with her husband, daughter, two cats, and dog.